WILFRED GRENFELL

HEROES OF THE CROSS

DAVID LIVINGSTONE

MARY SLESSOR

JOHN WESLEY

WILFRED GRENFELL

WILFRED GRENFELL

MARSHALLS

Marshall Morgan & Scott
31 Beggarwood Lane, Basingstoke, Hants

Copyright © Marshall Morgan & Scott

First published by Oliphants Ltd 1954

Reprinted 1955
Third impression 1962
First issued in paperback in Lakeland 1962
This edition 1982
Impression number 10 9 8 7 6 5 4 3 2

ISBN: 0 551 00944 6

Printed in Great Britain by Richard Clay (The Chaucer Press) Ltd,
Bungay, Suffolk

CONTENTS

LABRADOR AND NEWFOUNDLAND

IF you get out an atlas and look at a map of the North American continent, you will find that the most easterly part of Canada is an area called Labrador. In size it is about as large as the British Isles, but in the whole of it there live only about as many people as would be found in this country in a small town. Many of these people are Eskimos. The others are either roving Indians or white people, whose ancestors have settled in the region.

Mention of Eskimos will make you think that Labrador is a very cold land and you will be right. Yet, if you are interested in geography you will notice that Labrador is no further from the Equator than are the British Isles. The reason for the great cold is that its shores are washed by a very cold sea current flowing down from the direction of the North Pole. We fortunately live in a land whose shores are warmed by a current which comes from near the Equator.

The 5,000 or so people who live in Labrador have a hard struggle to make a living. Most of them are fishermen. A few are hunters, who trap animals in order to obtain furs out of which the fur coats are made which you see ladies wearing in the winter.

For many years no one troubled themselves about these people or their welfare. This book is the story of a doctor, a very brave man who chose to spend his life among them rather than to practise in more comfortable surroundings. His name was Doctor Wilfred Grenfell. Because of the splendid work he did for the people of Labrador he was honoured with a Knighthood and is, therefore, often called Sir Wilfred Grenfell. So closely was his life linked with the people of the far-off corner of the British Commonwealth that to most people he is known as Grenfell of Labrador.

Before you close your atlas I want you to notice that to the South of Labrador and separated from it by a channel called Belle Isle (Beautiful Isle) Strait is an island known as Newfoundland. This is the oldest part of the British Commonwealth, having been discovered in 1497 by a great sailor and explorer named John Cabot. This island is about the size of England and is, for the most part, much warmer than Labrador and is the home of well over 300,000 people. The island is shaped like a triangle and along one side (the North) it is cold and bleak, while the other parts of the island enjoy a comparatively mild climate. Among the fishermen living on that bleak side of the island Doctor Grenfell did a great deal of his work, so that he is honoured in Newfoundland as highly as in Labrador.

Since 1949 Newfoundland has been merged with Canada, but before then it was an independent Dominion, proud to call itself the oldest Dominion in the British Commonwealth. Labrador belonged to Newfoundland, although it was part of the mainland adjoining Canada. Those of you who are stamp collectors know that Newfoundland used to have its own stamps. When Grenfell died the Government showed how much they thought of him by issuing a stamp which shows him on his little ship, the *Strathcona*.

Now, having learned a little about the lands where Grenfell spent the greater part of his life, we are ready to hear about the man himself and what made him leave England to work among the folk of Labrador.

II

BOYHOOD DAYS

WILFRED GRENFELL was born on February 28th, 1865, at a seaside place in Cheshire called Parkgate. It was not a leap year of course. Had it been he would have narrowly missed being one of those who only get a birthday every four years!

Near his home the River Dee flows into the sea. There is a wide estuary, with miles of sand on either side of the river. Here he spent many wonderful hours with his older brother, especially during school holidays. His father was headmaster of a boarding school and when the boys went home for their holidays he and his wife often went abroad, leaving the two boys in the care of the school matron. Because of this they had much more freedom than did most boys of eighty years ago and indeed more than many do to-day. They came to know every inch of the sands of the Dee and made friends with the fisherfolk who lived in the neighbourhood. Often the boys went out in the fishing vessels and stayed away for a day and a night at a time.

Another attraction on the sands was the large number of unusual birds which were to be seen there—sandpipers, king plovers, curlews, wild ducks and many others. Sometimes the boys took an old gun with them and tried their hand at shooting. Wilfred soon became a good shot and having no dog, would swim out to collect the birds he had killed. Often he went out on his own, the two boys—like a good many other brothers—did not always get on well together. Then he would wander for miles, losing all sense of time and even forgetting to eat. On his eighth birthday wading out for some birds he had shot, he fell head over heels into a deep hole and lost his gun.

Once, just after his parents had gone away for their usual holiday, the boys thought they would invite a cousin who lived in London to visit them. They, therefore, sent him a telegram, "Dear Sid. Come down and stay the holidays. Father has gone to Aix." Next day they received a reply which read. "Not gone yet. Father"! It turned out that their parents had broken their journey and stayed the night at the very house to which the boys' telegram had been sent.

On Sundays the boys would go to church. In those days it was the custom for the preachers to speak at great length and the boys found the services wearisome and boring. One Sunday their patience evidently became exhausted and a complaint was made to their father that they had chalked pictures on the pew in front and had coated chocolate on the hot pipes!

On reaching fourteen the boys were sent away to school, Wilfred to Marlborough and his brother to Repton, where he got into so much trouble that he was given a second chance at Clifton.

Some of the things which went on at Marlborough in those days sound strange to us. Beer was served with the dinner and the boys were allowed as much of it as they wanted. A common punishment was the writing out of lines and Doctor Grenfell tells of doing these in advance during school time so that he would not have to give up any time that might be devoted to games! There was a good deal of bullying, but the customary method of settling an argument was by boxing, which took place each evening after 10 p.m.

When he was sixteen Wilfred Grenfell spent a time in the sick-room with a troublesome cough. The school doctor thought the boy was worse than he really was and the result was that for several months Wilfred lived in the South of France where the winter is warmer than in England.

Grenfell did well at games and at his studies. He passed examinations without any trouble. Among his friends was a boy who, though extremely clever at mathematics and chemistry, had no interest in games whatever. Most of the boys would make fun of him in the rough manner of those days, once hitting him on the forehead with a large lump of coal. Grenfell protected his friend from the bullies as far as possible and in the holiday time went to stay with him in North Wales, where the days were spent in the kind of life he most enjoyed—swimming, boating, rock-climbing and shooting.

His parents taught him that the only excuse for killing birds or animals was the achievement of some purpose. Thus he did not kill for the sake of killing. Many of the birds he shot, he afterwards stuffed. He and his brother between them made useful and interesting collections of birds' eggs, butterflies, moths, seaweeds and flowers. Thus was knowledge gained which was to prove useful later on.

III

CHOOSING A CAREER

WHEN Grenfell was eighteen his father asked him one day what he was going to be. Strangely enough, it was a question to which he had never given any thought. It was usual in those days for a boy to follow in the footsteps of his father or uncles. He did not, however, want to become a clergyman. The Army might have appealed to him, for among his ancestors were many who had distinguished themselves on the field of battle, among them Sir Richard Grenville, who in the days of the first Queen Elizabeth won ever-lasting fame for his bravery against enormous odds. You have probably read how in his little ship the *Revenge* he fought against fifty-three

Spanish vessels. More recently an uncle had served with distinction in the Siege of Lucknow. So many of his relatives were in the Indian Army that on one occasion, in Delhi, forty-eight of his cousins met at an important function.

It was a visit of the family doctor, however, which turned Grenfell's mind towards medicine. The sight of a pickled human brain in a large jar so thrilled him that he made up his mind to become a doctor.

At about this time his father decided to leave Cheshire and he accepted the appointment of chaplain at the London Hospital, which at the time was the largest hospital in the British Isles.

Attached to the hospital was a training school for those studying to become doctors. We might expect that such students would have to put in a great deal of serious work—they certainly have to now—but in those days no one seemed to bother and the lectures were treated light-heartedly. Grenfell tells us that he only attended two botany lectures the whole time he was there. At the first, someone had spilt a strong smelling liquid over the lecturer's platform and the lecture never took place. At the second, two pigeons were let loose in the room and the so-called students shot at them with pea-shooters! The chemistry professor was often pelted with peas and would leave the lecture room in despair. Grenfell's chief interest at the time was in sport and, according to the season, he spent most of his spare time at cricket, football or rowing. In the sports he won second place at throwing the hammer. During his one and only term at Oxford he played football for the University and for three years he played for Richmond.

He had been at the Hospital for about two years when there occurred an event which was to shape the rest of his life. He had been out to see a patient and coming back to the Hospital he passed a large tent and went to see what was happening. He found a service in progress and when a gentleman began a long and boring prayer, Grenfell got up to go. At that moment, however, another gentleman called out, "Let us sing a hymn while our brother finishes his prayer". The speaker was an American evangelist, D. L. Moody, and he realized that people would soon go away if they were bored. Grenfell stayed. He was deeply impressed by the evangelist's message. He went home that night determined either to live his life as a doctor as Christ would do or to have nothing further to do with religion. Soon afterwards he went to another service at which two brothers spoke, J. E. K. and C. T. Studd. Both were famous cricketers who had decided to spend their lives in the service of Christ. When they asked for those who wished to follow Christ to stand, a lad dressed as a sailor stood up boldly. Grenfell, who had rarely known what it was to be afraid of anything before, feared to stand; but, after seeing the sailor boy's courage, he stood.

At once he began to do Christian work. He started by taking a class of boys in a local Sunday-school. On Sunday evenings he went out with a young Australian doctor and held services among some of the poorest and roughest folk in London. For the first time in his life he found himself among people who were really poor. Sometimes one of the young doctors would have to sit on someone who had had too much to drink and was making such a noise that they could not make themselves heard. Most of the people they spoke to welcomed them and recognized that the young doctors were trying to help them.

He arranged boxing classes for the boys of the Sunday-school, believing that boxing was an ideal sport for teaching them to play fair and to enjoy the fun whether they won or lost.

Sometimes Grenfell met with serious opposition, but his fitness and strength stood him in good stead. On one occasion an unfriendly crowd closed in around him, intending to force some whisky down his throat. By using methods learned on the football field he soon scattered his opponents and left them in confusion!

Whenever possible, Grenfell spent his time at the sea. North Wales was a favourite resort. From there he sailed with his brother and two others in a small boat, intending to cross to Ireland. When they reached Douglas in the Isle of Man they went ashore to visit places of interest on the island. He was barelegged and brown from the sun when a lady stopped him and asked if he was an Eskimo! Another time they sailed through the Menai Straits and made for Milford Haven in South Wales, a journey which took them close to many dangerous rocks. They visited old castles, climbed Snowdon and had numerous adventures. Fishing, shooting, swimming and rowing—all were experiences which were to be useful in the future.

Getting back to London, Grenfell told his boys there of the fun he had had on holiday and the thought struck him that his Christianity would be more effective if he did something to help these boys to enjoy such a holiday. The next summer he took thirteen of them to North Wales. They slept in tents on a deserted point of the coast, and we can imagine what a good time they had. One night the boys visited the station in Bangor and, taking some labels which they found, plastered them all over the baggage on the platform!

The camp rules were simple but had to be kept strictly. As few clothes as necessary were worn. Every boy had to have a swim before breakfast. Some of them did not get anything to eat until nearly dinner time! They had to learn to swim before they were allowed out in the boats. Needless to say, the camp was a great success. There were thirty boys the second year and nearly a hundred the third year. Each year the boys climbed Snowdon, which is the highest mountain in England and Wales. After several visits to North Wales, the camp was held at Lulworth in Dorset and the boys were able to explore the lovely coastline between Swanage and Weymouth.

Among the surgeons at the London Hospital was one who, like Grenfell, was a great lover of the sea and of sailing. His name was Sir Frederick

Treves. Every Boxing Day he used to sail across the English Channel to France.

One day he sent for the young Doctor Grenfell and told him that a doctor was needed to sail with the fishing fleet in the North Sea. Hundreds of little fishing vessels were away from land for weeks at a time. As many as twenty thousand men would be on the ships, with no doctor to help them if taken ill before returning to port. A group of people had founded a Mission to Deep Sea Fishermen. The Mission had its own boat which went out with the fleet. On one side of this boat— the starboard side for those of you who know a little about ships—was carved in large letters the text, "Heal the sick"; on the port side were the words, "Preach the word", while round the brass rim of the wheel was written, "Jesus said, 'Follow Me and I will make you fishers of men'." This vessel would visit as many fleets as possible during a voyage.

It was just the kind of life which Doctor Grenfell loved. He tells us that he enjoyed every hour of the long trip. He found himself among a cheerful, merry crowd of men and boys, who laughed at danger and appeared not to mind the discomforts of their lives. Many of them in those days could not read or write. Few of the vessels carried the instruments by which ships at sea find their way about. But so well did the skippers know the North Sea that they would let down the lead cups and bring up a sample of gravel from the sea bed, from study of which they knew well enough where

they were and could find their way home. As I
expect you know, the North Sea is very shallow.
Such methods would not be possible in deeper
waters, nor among men who had not known the
sea all their lives.

Many of the boys on the fishing vessels were
orphans and one of the objects of the Mission was
to get someone at home to write regular letters to
such lads and to meet them when the vessels
returned to port.

Not all the fishing trips were in the North Sea
area. Sometimes Doctor Grenfell found himself on
the Irish coast. Once he was called to a patient in
a lighthouse, built on a rock called Fastnet, standing
alone out in the great Atlantic Ocean. The sea was
too rough for the doctor to land on the rock. His
boat came in as close as possible; then a line was
thrown from a high crane in the lighthouse. The
doctor fastened the rope round his waist and
immediately found himself swinging through the
air until he was pulled into the lighthouse by a
trapdoor. When the patient had been attended to,
he returned to the boat by the same method.

IV

ACROSS THE ATLANTIC

WHEN Doctor Grenfell was twenty-seven, he was
asked by the Mission to cross the Atlantic to find
out whether the kind of work being done off the
shores of Britain could be done in other fishing

grounds. To cross an ocean 3,000 miles wide in a small vessel was just the kind of adventure which appealed to the doctor and in June, 1892, he sailed for Newfoundland. So rough were the seas and so strong the wind that the skipper decided to take shelter in an Irish port called Crookhaven, where they met some old friends who had been among the doctor's patients on a previous visit. They were given numerous presents of eggs and green vegetables as signs of good-will. When they continued their journey, the winds were against them and slowed them down. On the 12th day out they came into thick fog and also saw their first icebergs. For five days they had to sail with great care. Then the fog lifted and in front of them could be seen a green and beautiful coastline. It was Newfoundland. They soon found out exactly where they were, a little to the north of the Harbour of St. John's, the capital of the island. When they came within sight of St. John's, the buildings were hidden by huge clouds of smoke. The city was on fire and the little vessel which, for days, had been in the cold region of the iceberg, found itself surrounded by great heat. Hundreds of people were made homeless, but Doctor Grenfell was amazed by the cheerfulness of the people in the face of their dreadful losses.

A few days after this the doctor was at sea again, sailing up the coast of Labrador with the fishing fleet. This gave him the first sight of the land which will always be linked with his own name. When he came to write his life story he

called it "A Labrador Doctor". His first sight of
the coast was on a sunny day in August. The sea
was as blue as the sky; scores of icebergs of all
shapes and sizes floated on the water; birds that he
had never seen before flew above him. It was a
day he never forgot as long as he lived. From
that day on he felt what he called "the lure of
Labrador". A lure is a bait. He meant that just as
a fish is attracted to the bait on the end of a line,
so he was attracted to this strange land.

He was not the first Christian missionary to go
among the Eskimos of Labrador; but he was the
first doctor, and he found plenty of work waiting
to be done.

One incident in particular occurred about
which he could not do much at the time, but
which made him realize how great was the need
of these people for good hospitals and medical
treatment. Their vessel was in a harbour called
Domino Run. He noticed a rough boat there
which was really not much more than a few
boards fastened together. A man was sitting in it,
dressed in a few rags which showed that he was
very poor. Presently the man spoke.

"Be you a real doctor?" he asked.

"That's what I call myself," replied Grenfell.

"Us hasn't got no money," the Eskimo went on,
"but there's a very sick man ashore, if so be you'd
come and see him."

A few minutes later the doctor found himself in
just about the meanest dwelling he had ever seen
in his life. Pebbles from the beach made up the

floor; bits of broken glass served for a window; the walls were damp. In this draughty and uncomfortable hut were half a dozen bunks, made of wood one above the other. The only furniture was a tiny stove. In a corner six children huddled, looking frightened at the sight of the stranger. A very sick man sat in the lower bunk coughing almost continuously, while a woman was giving him cold water to drink with a wooden spoon. It was a touching sight.

As he took in the tragic scene, Doctor Grenfell felt very helpless. The man was suffering from something called pneumonia and probably another disease even more serious. He needed hospital treatment, but if they took him on board the little hospital vessel, the chances were that he would never come back to his home and family. It was the fishing season and the man was too ill to go out to earn a living for himself and his family. A few weeks later he died, leaving the children and their mother in dreadful poverty. Doctor Grenfell thought of the Christians in England with their comfortable homes, good food and warm clothes. They must be told and they must be made to realize that they alone could do something to make the lives of these folk easier. He had found a task, a man's task, which was to occupy him for the rest of his life.

There were many other incidents which made him remember that first visit to Labrador. They even had a wedding on board the Mission vessel.

As for the scenery, he had never seen anything

so attractive before. There were the mysterious fjords—long, narrow arms of the sea, with high cliffs on either side; hundreds of islands which had never been shown on any maps; strange birds, berries and flowers, unknown except on these rugged shores; and the queerest rocks, cliffs and boulders that you could expect to find anywhere.

Sometimes a fisherman would bring him a stone arrowhead he had found—evidence that the Viking sailors had been there long before Columbus and Cabot had crossed the great ocean to find the American continent. You have probably heard of these old time sailors who, nearly one thousand years ago, sailed from Iceland to Greenland and then on to North America, but whose discoveries were so completely forgotten that even Columbus himself thought he was going to find India on the Western side of the Atlantic. These Vikings had sailed down the Labrador coast, had landed in places, and had left behind them these pieces of evidence which show that they had been there.

The splendid work done by Doctor Grenfell on this first trip among the Labrador fishermen was realized by all who knew about it. The Governor of Newfoundland called a special meeting to thank him and to say that he hoped the Mission would be able to go on with the work which had been begun.

V

AMONG THE MORAVIANS

WHEN it was known in London how much had
been done and how great was the need for
doctors among the folk of Labrador, a great effort
was made to go on with the work. The next year
Doctor Grenfell was back again, taking two more
doctors with him and two nurses. On the way
over there they were playing cricket on deck.
Somebody hit the ball over the side into the sea.
It was the last ball they had and in his anxiety to
get it back Grenfell jumped into the sea after it,
shouting at the man at the helm to wait for him.
You will be glad to know that he found the ball
and was soon hauled on board again.

With more helpers, it was now possible to set up
hospitals where some of the worst cases could get
proper attention. Two islands, two hundred
miles apart were chosen, both of them in areas
where large numbers of fishing vessels gathered.
Their names were Battle Harbour at the mouth of
the St. Lawrence River and Indian Harbour on
the Atlantic. At Battle Harbour they had the use
of a building belonging to a fishery firm. At
Indian Harbour a building had to be put up but
this was done for them by the fishery firm which
owned the harbour.

Leaving one of the other doctors in charge of
the hospital ship, Doctor Grenfell sailed up the

coast in a tiny vessel, only eight feet wide, to a
place called Okkak. No coal could be obtained
for the boat's engine and wood was used instead.
It was a real adventure for him to sail those seas
in this tiny vessel. It was a boat which he had
found near his home in Cheshire. He and a friend
had repaired it and had steamed it to Liverpool
where it was hoisted aboard a larger ship for the
crossing of the Atlantic. When they reached
Newfoundland the funnel of their little vessel was
nowhere to be found. It had become mixed up with
the baggage in the hold and they had to wait for
a new one before they could start out.

He ran short of wood for the boiler and had to
burn the top of the cabin to get enough steam up
to complete his trip. Repairs delayed him also and
another steamer was sent out to search for him.
However the voyage ended safely and a great
deal of useful information had been collected.

It was during this trip that Doctor Grenfell
met some other missionaries who had gone to
Labrador to preach the Good News to the
Eskimos. These people were Moravians and they
came from Germany. The story of the Moravians
is one which you must read for yourselves some day.
The movement began when a young nobleman
saw a beautiful painting of Christ on the Cross
and felt that he *must* do something for One who had
loved him so much as to die for him. He gathered
around him other earnest Christians and they
sent out missionaries to places where other
Christians had never even thought of going.

Some became slaves to work among the slaves in the West Indies. Others went to the remote lands of Labrador and Tibet. This was 130 years before Doctor Grenfell reached Labrador; and though they had built five mission stations, they had never had a doctor there. Of course, there was plenty of medical work to be done and he had a busy time. His journey took him where no Englishman had ever been before, among mountains and cliffs, rivers and bays, scenery which he loved. At night he and his companion would go ashore to collect specimens of strange flowers and capture birds or fish for their meals.

On Sundays the Eskimos who had become Christians would put on spotlessly clean clothes and meet together to worship God. The Moravians had taught them to read and write, although there were no books for them except the few they had written or translated themselves.

Translation from one language to another is interesting work, but is rather difficult when one comes to a word for which the other language has no parallel word. The Eskimos, for instance, had no words for "God" or "love". The Moravians then used the German words and tried to explain their meaning. When they came to the text about Christ being "the Lamb of God", they called Him "the White Seal of God", for no Eskimos would have known what a lamb was like. An old lady who heard of this sent Doctor Grenfell a toy lamb, rather the worse for wear and tear, with a note saying, "sent in order that the heathen may know better"!

The doctor enjoyed the singing and music of these Eskimos. He was able to record their voices and you can perhaps imagine how excited they were when the record was played back to them. Another cause of excitement was the magic lantern. Sometimes the Eskimos tried to catch hold of the pictures on the slides. Some slides were made showing the Eskimos themselves. Great was the confusion when one was shown them on which was an old woman who had died since the photograph had been taken. They quite thought she had come back to life again!

I expect you have sometimes met people who think that the number thirteen is unlucky, while as for "Friday the 13th" they think that all kinds of dreadful things are likely to happen on such a date. We call such people superstitious. The simple people of almost every race on earth have their own superstitions, which we can smile about, though we should feel sorry that they know no better.

Doctor Grenfell found many strange superstitious beliefs among the people of Labrador. They would hang up the head of a wolf or fox as a kind of a barometer, believing that the wind would blow from whichever direction the head faced. But if they hung a seal's head they thought it would face away from the wind.

The doctor once met an old seaman who proudly claimed that he never suffered from boils because he always cut his nails on Monday! Another superstition connected with finger nails was a belief that asthma could be cured by allowing the nails to grow long and then cutting them with sharp scissors. Once, when examining a patient, he found that he had a bone from a haddock hanging round his neck. It was a charm against rheumatism. Sugar was believed to be a cure for bad eyes and if a baby was troubled with his eyes, the parents would blow sugar into them.

Doctor Grenfell took a great liking to these simple people, whom he found to be always cheerful, although living in great poverty in one of the coldest parts of the earth. It was not unusual for people to starve to death in a land where there was little food apart from fish. Once some pigs, being hungry, broke into a church and ate the Bible!

The people of Labrador not only face cold and poverty, but danger. It is not uncommon for men to be carried out to sea on a small iceberg— or icepan as it is called. When an epidemic such as influenza broke out the people died in large numbers. Too often, when the doctor arrived, he would find that he was too late to prevent tragedy.

Once, when cruising along the coast, he anchored near two lonely islands. Almost immediately he was called to the bedside of a dying girl. He found a very pretty girl of about eighteen years of age, the only woman among a crowd of men, doing the cooking and mending for them. For more than a fortnight she had been in bed. The old sea captain, whose servant she was, had looked after her tenderly but had not washed her or changed the bedclothes. The doctor knew there was little hope of saving her life, but he was determined to do what he could. Within a short time he had the poor girl washed and laid in clean clothes, in which she slept peacefully. At about midnight, however, she died.

As her death had been caused by something which could easily be caught by others, it was decided to burn everything which had belonged to her and which she had been using. The doctor and the sea captain carried her belongings out to the edge of the cliff, where they lit such a bonfire as made them think of Guy Fawkes night at home. It was a foggy night and a boatload of fishermen, among them the captain's son, were out on the waters, uncertain of their position. Suddenly through the fog they saw the light of the bonfire and were guided to safety.

So well did the work progress that before long it was decided to keep the hospital going right through the cold Labrador winter, when everything is frozen up and normal life becomes impossible. At first Doctor Grenfell had thought that this could not be done, but so many of the Eskimos pleaded with him to do so that it was decided to try it out and a Doctor Willway offered to stay. When Grenfell returned the following summer it was in fear that his friend might have changed so much that they would hardly recognize him. It was a pleasant surprise therefore, when Doctor Willway appeared, looking so fit and well that they felt more jealous of his good fortune than sympathy for the hardships he had endured.

VI

THE SEAL HUNTERS

ANOTHER adventure in which Doctor Grenfell shared during his first few years in Labrador was a trip with seal hunters. He did not really like the idea of hunting and killing hundreds of seals. They breed more slowly than most other animals and are needed by the Eskimos who can find a useful purpose for every part of a seal, in providing themselves with food and clothing.

However, a fleet of seal hunters was going out; a doctor was needed and Grenfell decided to go. He loved adventure and he knew only too well that these men daily risked their lives in their unusual occupation. He knew of some who had been marooned for thirty six hours on a floating pan of ice before the wind changed and carried them to safety. Even then they had to make a long journey over the ice before they reached land, more dead than alive. He knew, also, of a boy who, with his father and two others had drifted out to sea in a small boat during a snowstorm. The boy's father and the other two had died from the cold but the boy had put on the clothes of the three dead men to keep himself warm. After drifting for seven days he heard a passing ship, called out, was heard and rescued.

The captain of the ship on which Doctor Grenfell sailed had had his share of adventure.

Once he had been on a ship which had picked up nineteen people, two of them women and one a baby, who had been afloat on icepans for five months. The baby had been born on the icepan.

One of the problems of the seal hunters is keeping warm. They cannot wear thick clothing, for it hampers them in jumping from one piece of ice to another. They often cut or sprain themselves. One day Doctor Grenfell decided to join in the fun himself. Slipping over the side of the ship on to a piece of ice he tried to get to the distant hunters, but he found that it was a slow process. After a time he reached a group of about a dozen men, but darkness came on and their ship was out of sight. To keep warm, they played leapfrog and other games which kept them moving. They ate what food they had and then tried to attract attention by lighting a fire. Sometime about the middle of the night they were rescued and had to face an angry captain who spoke to them like a headmaster telling off some mischievous schoolboys.

One morning some of the men were out looking for seals when they came upon a party of survivors from a ship which had been crushed to pieces between the icepans. They were Eskimos and they had to walk at least a hundred miles, some as much as three hundred miles, back to their homes. These brave hunters and fishermen were the kind of men for whom Doctor Grenfell was glad to do anything. He would have found no pleasure in the comforts of a life in England to compare with the joy of sharing the hardships of

these courageous folk. And not only did he care
for their bodies, to tend them when injured or ill.
He was also concerned with the more important
part of a man's being which we call his soul. He
had with him on the expedition a number of hymn
books and on the Sunday afternoons—no seals are
ever hunted on Sundays—they lay on the deck
singing the praises of God and talking about the
more important things of life. "For my part", he
wrote, "I felt the nearness of God's presence as
really as I have felt it in the mysterious environ-
ment of the most magnificent cathedral. Eternal
life seemed so close, as if it lay just over the
horizon of ice, in the eternal blue beyond".

VII

ICELAND

ANOTHER land which Doctor Grenfell visited
about this time was Iceland. This large island in
the North Atlantic is even further North than
Labrador and lies only just outside the Arctic
Circle. It is not so cold, however, as Labrador because it gains some benefit from the famous warm
current which we call the Gulf Stream. Its capital
is a place called Reykjavik, a name which means
"smoking village". It is so called because hot
streams come out of the ground near the town. The
steam from these streams looks like smoke always
rising from the earth's surface.

You have probably learned in your geography

lessons that in some parts of the world, in the far
North and the far South, the days are so long in
the summer that for a time there is no night at all,
while in the winter, the opposite happens and for
months on end there is no daylight. Well, Iceland is
so far north that in the summer there is hardly any
night. Doctor Grenfell found this rather confusing
because it was so easy to forget the time. Sometimes he found that it was the middle of the night,
while he had been thinking it was still evening!
It was even difficult to think what day it was.

The reason for this visit to Iceland, as you have
probably guessed, was to arrange for medical
attention and Christian witness among the men
of the fishing fleets. It was an area where fish were
plentiful. So many were being caught that the
men threw back the cod and haddock into the
water, because they were less valuable than the
plaice and other fish being netted. As these fish
were used to swimming far below the surface they
were taken by surprise when they found themselves
thrown back into the sea. Before they could get
used to this change, they were an easy prey for gulls
and other birds. The doctor found that a Mission
vessel was certainly needed in the area, though it
would prove more difficult work than in other fishing grounds, because the fleets were so scattered.

After this trip, Doctor Grenfell spent a well-
deserved holiday in the Scilly Isles, off Lands'
End, in the extreme South-west corner of England.
He went to stay with Sir Frederick Treves, the
surgeon under whom he had studied at the

London Hospital and who had encouraged him to become a doctor among the fishermen. Another visitor at the same time was Sir Frederick's nephew, Mr. A. E. W. Mason. You may have heard of him, for he has written some very good books of adventure. One day during their visit there was a carnival, which included a display of life-saving by local swimmers. Doctor Grenfell and Mr. Mason decided that they would make the carnival a little more interesting. They went off and dressed themselves up, Mr. Mason as an old lady and the Doctor as an aged clergyman in an old fashioned hat trimmed with beaver fur and called a beaver hat. In this strange disguise Mr. Mason fell off the pier into the water. Doctor Grenfell pulled his huge hat down over his head and dived in after the "old lady". You can imagine what excitement there was among the real life-savers and the spectators. The two men were dragged out of the sea. Mr. Mason lost his skirt in the confusion and ran off in a bonnet and bathing suit! To crown the joke the local paper wrote the story of what had happened as though it really was an old lady who had been rescued!

Back at work again after his holiday in the Scilly Isles, the doctor found himself once more among the fishing fleets in the North Sea. One day he had a patient who said he had taken poison. It turned out that he had gone to the doctor for some medicine for a cough and also for some liniment to rub in to his skipper's leg. Somehow he got the two bottles mixed up, so that the skipper rubbed the cough mixture into his leg, while the other man drank the liniment. Fortunately it was not poison, but they could not persuade the man that he would not die. He was put on the hospital ship and given nothing except water and castor oil. Evidently he did not like this, for the next day he felt better!

In the following spring they heard that their ship off the Labrador coast had been caught in an ice floe and had been crushed to pieces. Fortunately no one had been on board at the time, but a new ship had to be found. Generous friends came forward to give the money needed for the new vessel. Chief of these was Lord Strathcona, and the new ship, launched on June 27th, 1899, was named after him. As she went down the slipway into the water, a band played "Eternal Father, strong to save", "God save the Queen", and "A Life on the Ocean Wave"! She was a fine vessel, larger than the famous *Golden Hind* in which, as you probably know, Drake sailed round the world.

VIII

THE FAMOUS DOGS

EVERYONE has heard of the Labrador Dogs. They are fine looking animals, measuring more than six feet from nosetip to tail. Tawny in colour, they have large bushy tails which they always carry erect. They are very strong and can pull heavy loads for long distances. They are much more like

wolves than most breeds of dogs. They howl like
wolves and have been known to kill and eat
human beings. They are afraid of nothing and will
even attack polar bears if they get the chance. They
do not mind how cold it is. Even with ice forming
all over their fur and their breath freezing so that
they cannot see the track, they do not seem to mind.

They also have a wonderful sense of direction;
that means being able to find the way even though
there is no track to follow. One spring the Doctor
had to travel seventy miles across country over a
track which had not been used for several months.
Nothing could be seen which would help him to
find the right way—in any case he had never
been that way before—but the leading dog had
been across once before in weather that was so bad
that the journey had taken three days. It involved
crossing several frozen lakes and making a path
through woods. As far as the Doctor knew, the
dog led the way without any mistake. At any
rate the journey only took twelve hours, including
a one-and-a-half hours rest.

The distance which the dogs can travel in a day
may vary from as little as five miles to as much as
seventy-five miles, according to the weather and
conditions. Normal travelling speed is about six
miles an hour, but in good conditions nearly ten
miles an hour can be done. Over short distances
the Doctor sometimes used a Straits dog, an
animal which is faster and less wolf-like than the
Labrador, but not so well able to endure a long
journey with a heavy load.

The dogs are useful, too, when hunting. One dog which the doctor had was called Podge and he was trained both to fetch birds shot down and to dive for seals. A friend of the Doctor's was once travelling across the ice with his dogs when a bear crossed the path of the sleigh and turned to attack the dogs. Quickly he cut the traces with his hunting knife and then while the dogs kept the bear's attention he was able to get his rifle and shoot the attacker.

The type of sleigh which the dogs pull is called a Komatik. It is eleven feet long and is made from a kind of wood, black spruce, which is both light and very strong.

The problem of keeping warm is not solved by wearing several layers of thick clothes. As you probably know, our bodies produce warmth and we keep warm if we can prevent that warmth from escaping. It is important the tunic should have a headpiece attached so that the heat cannot escape through the neck. Boots of sealskin and deerskin are made by Eskimo women who chew the skin to soften it before sewing with deer sinew. I am afraid this habit does no good to their teeth, for most of the women lose them early in life. Little Eskimo girls are brought up to chew these skins and are very clever at doing so.

An important item to carry when travelling is an axe. It is sometimes needed to clear a track ahead of the dogs.

One day in the middle of the winter an urgent call came from the father of a family of eight who had had an accident with his gun. It had gone off while his right hand was over the muzzle. To stop the bleeding he had put his hand into a barrel of flour, but poison found its way into the blood and spread up the man's elbow. They brought him to the hospital and then began a fight for his life. The man would have preferred death to the loss of his arm, but it took many weeks before he was out of danger. Even then skin was needed for his hand, and this was supplied partly by Doctor Grenfell himself and partly by another Doctor.

The next winter an old lady was brought in by sleigh with a diseased leg. The leg had to be taken off, but no money was available to buy an artificial one for her. Shortly afterwards Doctor Grenfell visited America and let people know of her need. Two people came forward with gifts of wooden legs, one of which exactly fitted.

On one occasion the doctor travelled with his dogs to visit a patient in a distant and lonely spot. The patient was too ill to come out when the doctor arrived, but asked him to shut his dogs up if they were vicious, where they could not harm a sheep which the man owned. The dogs had hauled a heavy sledge for fifty miles and must have been very hungry.

One of the dogs was a fine animal called Kite. Later, he was to save the Doctor's life. He was not vicious but possessed a hearty appetite and Doctor Grenfell thought it would be wisest to put him in an outhouse.

The following morning the patient was well

enough to come to see the Doctor off. When he went to the outhouse to get his dog, the man called out to him not to open the door as his sheep was in there. Of course, the Doctor had to open the door. When he did so, he found no sheep, only a very contented looking dog, which had put on so much weight during the night that he could not walk!

IX

BATTLE AGAINST POVERTY

ONE of Doctor Grenfell's greatest worries in the early days of the work was the system of trading in Labrador. It was the custom of the fishermen who lived on the coast to bring all their catch to a merchant, who, in return, would supply them with food, clothes and other goods. This may sound quite harmless, but the fishermen had a strange habit of wanting a little more than the value of the catch. In this way they felt they were getting their money's worth. But it also meant they put themselves into the power of the trader. From him they hired their nets for fishing and traps for hunting; and to him they were then obliged to turn over their catch. To Doctor Grenfell the system was not very different from slavery in which human beings are the property of their masters.

His duty as a Christian Doctor did not end when he had preached the Gospel and attended the sick. He wanted to improve the way in which these people lived and he believed that this could be done by getting them to share their responsibilities. One year, at a village called Red Bay, the people felt they could no longer manage to earn a living and asked to be moved further south. Seventeen families between them had only been able to save about £20 during a whole year. Doctor Grenfell arranged for them to borrow some money to start a co-operative store. They were then able to buy the goods they needed. Soon they repaid the loan and the new scheme worked so well that they were able to keep out of debt, even in the bad years when very few fish were caught.

Another effort made to help the people by providing them with work other than fishing was the putting up of a saw mill. The mill was taken from England in parts and put together on the spot like a huge jig-saw puzzle.

Yet another venture was a fox farm near the hospital at St. Anthony. Red, white and silver foxes were caught to start the farm. On the way, on board the *Strathcona* they became very tame. They played with the dogs, fell down the companion way and always seemed to be getting under the sailors' feet and yelping as their tails were trodden on! The white and silver foxes were rather shy, but the red ones liked to be hugged and squeezed, squealing with delight whenever anyone thus took notice of them.

The fox farm was not easy to run. In the early days many of the foxes died or were eaten by their parents. But Doctor Grenfell's venture was the first of several in Newfoundland and Labrador.

X

COLLECTING CHILDREN

ALL boys and girls are collectors at some time or other. They collect stamps, bus tickets, pictures of cars, trains, footballers or the Queen, according to their fancy. Doctor Grenfell was no exception. You have heard how as a boy he formed collections of stamps, butterflies and birds' eggs. But in Labrador he began to collect children!

The collection began one day when he was visiting a village where there lived a boy and girl who had no parents. They were so poor that even the clothes they were wearing had been lent to them by people in the village. So great was the poverty in that place that the few families living there found it hard to feed and clothe their own children, let alone the two unfortunate orphans. Doctor Grenfell, therefore, brought them to England, where kind friends looked after them and made sure they were given a better start in life. They grew up to live happy and useful lives.

One day, the *Strathcona* was sailing close to shore when the watch saw a signal for help. The Doctor landed and in a lonely log house, where lived settlers from Scotland, he found the mother dead on the floor, the father dying and five small children sitting sadly on a heap of sand. By morning the father had died. They were victims of influenza, and the Doctor had five youngsters to care for.

On another occasion, when the ship was anchored near a group of islands, a woman came aboard carrying a bundle under each arm. She put the bundles on the doctor's table and began to untie them. Each bundle contained a small child and both the twins were blind. Soon he found out that she had four more children and that her husband had been killed in an accident with a gun.

"How do you manage to feed the babies?" the doctor asked.

"Indeed, I can't," the poor woman replied.

"Whatever are you going to do with them?"

"I'm going to give them to you, doctor."

Doctor Grenfell looked after the blind twins until they were old enough to go to a school for blind children in Halifax, Nova Scotia. Eventually their eyes were operated on and they became able to see colours and read large print. For a time they were teachers at one of the Mission outposts. One of them married a fisherman and became the mother of a fine boy, but, sad to say, he was born blind.

Some more children came under the Doctor's care from a deserted village which he visited. Looking into a log cabin, where there were no signs of life, one of his companions noticed a small face peering through a hole in the ceiling. It turned out that there were four children hiding in the loft. None of them had any clothes. Presently, a woman with a baby in her arms appeared. The story was that her husband had gone away three months before and there had been no news of him. She had been out looking for berries to feed her family.

"For God's sake," she said to the doctor, "take them and feed them. I can do no more."

It meant a journey of seven miles across open sea. Fortunately Doctor Grenfell had with him some lads fresh from college spending their holiday helping him with his work. They took off their own coats to cover the naked children.

The first Children's Home was built at the northern end of the island of Newfoundland. A second was later opened in Labrador itself at a place called Cartwright. It was not long before the Mission was caring for more than fifty children and had to enlarge its buildings.

The cost of a new building was carefully worked out and it was found that it would be about 25 cents (just over a shilling) for every brick. An appeal was then made to folk in Britain and America to give "bricks".

In addition to the boys and girls who had lost their parents or whose parents were unable to care for them properly, there was the problem of many more boys and girls who were growing up without any chance to go to school. Some of you may think that that would be very nice, but grown-ups who have never been to school spend most of their lives being sorry for having missed the opportunity which nearly everyone in the world now gets.

A boy of sixteen, a carpenter, offered to work for Doctor Grenfell for ten hours a day if he would spend one hour teaching him to read and write.

The only answer seemed to be to start Boarding Schools. Eventually there were four orphanage-boarding schools, and parents who could afford to do so paid something, while Christian friends in America and Britain found the rest of the money needed to run the schools.

Another great need that Doctor Grenfell discovered was for toys and games. There were none at all. Try to imagine little girls with no dolls. It is difficult, for nearly every race on the earth makes dolls of some kind for its children to play with. It did not take the doctor long to do something about the shortage, and soon a trunk full of dolls was on its way to Labrador. But instead of letting the children have them to play with, the grown-ups hung them out of their reach on the walls! They seemed to think that they were ornaments.

Next, the children had to be taught to play games—not games like football and cricket, but the more simple ones which in almost any other part of the world children invent themselves.

When the school time-table was planned, it was not like the time-table which you have at school. Doctor Grenfell could not see any good reason for teaching the boys and girls of Labrador such subjects as Latin and French. But there were very good reasons for teaching them how to cook, to repair boots and to tin salmon.

Another need was for books, not only for children but for the older folk as well. One day a white-haired old man rowed out to the Mission vessel and pleaded with the doctor to let him have a book to read. He only had two rather ancient history books and he had read them again and again. Soon he was rowing back to his home with a whole library of books to keep him busy until the vessel came that way again when he could change them for others.

Some of the cleverer boys and girls were sent to Canada or the United States to share the advantages offered by schools in those countries. It was always on condition that they went back to Labrador for at least two years afterwards. Most of them remained for the rest of their lives, not wanting the luxuries of warmer lands, when there was the opportunity to serve their own people as teachers, clergymen, carpenters, engineers and builders.

XI

SHIPWRECKS AND LIGHTHOUSES

You have probably heard people say that it is an ill wind that blows nobody any good. It is a way of saying that when a misfortune occurs, usually somebody gains something by it.

This is certainly true in Labrador whenever a ship is wrecked on the rocky and unfriendly coast. One of the first ships to be wrecked after Doctor Grenfell went out there was the s.s. *Mexico*, carrying a cargo of food supplies. Barrels of flour floated ashore along the coast, while for weeks afterwards fishermen went out to catch hams, cheeses, kegs of butter and all kinds of things! The sea for miles around was like a huge "lucky dip". To people who were very poor and often short of food, a shipwreck could be a most fortunate event.

One winter when there was a serious shortage of flour in Labrador, a large French steamer s.s. *Baucis* became stuck on a flat reef. The vessel did not sink, but remained stuck there. It was only necessary to bore a hole in the side of the ship and a stream of wheat would pour out.

Another ship to get wrecked was the s.s. *Bay Rupert*, a large steamer, belonging to the Hudson's Bay Company, and loaded with supplies for the trading posts in the far North from which the furs come from which many of the fur coats you see are made. The ship's lifeboats took the passengers to a desert island which for some reason was called "Farmyards", although no chickens had ever been on it until the survivors of the *Bay Rupert* arrived with several crates of them. From this wreck came a wonderful variety of treasures—sledges, gunpowder and guns, food of all kinds and chewing gum.

Large areas of these seas were not charted when Doctor Grenfell first went there and there were no lighthouses along the rugged coast, so that it is not surprising there were so many wrecks.

One summer Doctor Grenfell nearly lost the *Strathcona*. His little vessel was tightly pinned between the shore and an ice floe which had been driven inshore by a strong breeze. The current was moving the ship towards dangerous rocks and the propeller was damaged. In the end, when he had almost given up hope of saving his vessel, the tide swept them past the danger spot and out into the open sea where there was plenty of room.

The doctor again and again asked those responsible to put lights at the most needed places along the coast, but for years nothing was done. Finally he told friends about the matter and they gave him enough money to put up a lighthouse at a place called Battle Harbour. This light has helped thousands of fishermen and has undoubtedly saved many lives.

About a hundred miles further North was a place called Indian Tickle. Here, too, a light was badly needed. But the Government would do nothing until after one tragic night when some vessels, caught in thick fog and heavy seas, were wrecked.

In the year 1908 enormous damage was caused by a hurricane, that is, a very strong gale which suddenly changes direction. On the night before the hurricane broke, the Doctor had reason to think that a storm was brewing and sailed his vessel to the safest possible place. The next day, at a place called Indian Harbour, every fishing vessel was filled with water and sank. By the next morning the sea was calm again and the doctor sailed along the shore in search of vessels which might need his help. He saw the remains of wrecks all the way along the coast, forty-one of them altogether. At one little place, about forty miles from Indian Harbour, were sixteen wrecks. Survivors had put up rough shelters on the shore and their womenfolk were tidying up the shacks and cooking their meals just as though they had been at home.

One of the wrecks, the *Pendragon*, looked as if it could be saved. The owner was only too glad to sell it to the Doctor, who then set to work to free her from the rocks and banks of mud. When they did get her free she was leaking badly, but two men said they would stay up all night pumping the water out. A day or two later the Doctor sold the *Pendragon* for the same price he had paid for it, to a skipper who had lost a brand new boat and was in great distress. After this adventure, the *Strathcona* returned to Indian Harbour with more than fifty people who had been rescued.

Soon after this disaster, the Governor of Newfoundland and Labrador paid the coast a visit. Doctor Grenfell acted as his pilot but had the misfortune to run the Governor's steamer on to a sandbank. She was pulled off by the *Strathcona*, but the Governor would not then trust the Doctor to take him near enough to shore to make a survey of the sea-bed!

A great deal of surveying was carried out by Doctor Grenfell about this time, and he drew up maps which were to prove of enormous use to the fishing fleets and other vessels using those waters. The Royal Geographical Society showed their appreciation by awarding him a prize for his services and inviting him to lecture to them.

XII

ABOUT REINDEER AND CARIBOU

WHEN you visit a zoo I expect an animal you are especially interested to see is a reindeer. Not only do we connect him with our stories of Father Christmas but he is a fine looking beast with a most impressive pair of horns. These animals live in the far North of Europe, in a part of the world where most other animals could not exist. They are quite happy to sleep in the open even at the coldest times of the year; they find their own food—mosses and lichen, digging down through deep snow, if necessary, far more quickly than a man could dig with a spade, and always digging just where the moss is to be found.

If you have a stamp collection, you probably have seen the Newfoundland stamp which shows us an animal very much like a reindeer. It is called a caribou and is found in North Newfoundland and parts of Labrador. They are a little bigger than reindeer, but mix with them without apparently knowing the difference. They are gentle, timid animals, very much more friendly than cows or even horses. Doctor Grenfell once had a fawn that was so fond of him that it would jump overboard and swim after him when he rowed ashore.

Although so timid, the caribou will defend himself stoutly when attacked. Once the Doctor watched a large husky dog creeping up on one of the stags. The deer saw the enemy coming, stood on his hind legs and dealt the dog such a blow that he was sent flying and tried no more tricks.

The reindeer is one of the most useful of all animals. They can be used for hauling heavy loads. From their milk good butter and cheese are made. Their skins afford excellent protection for Eskimos who have to sleep out on the snow in the winter; and the leather made from their skins is used for moccasins and light, windproof clothes. Then reindeer meat is delicious to eat; strong thread is made from their sinews, and as the sinews swell when wet, this thread is ideal for sewing the canoe coverings as it ensures that they become quite watertight.

Another advantage about them is that they breed more quickly than cattle. When their numbers are not kept under control, the herds can become very large indeed.

I have said enough about these wonderful animals for you to realize how useful they might be to the people of Labrador, where the numbers of caribou once fell so seriously that there was real danger of the species dying out. Following his policy of doing everything possible to make life easier for the Eskimos, Doctor Grenfell asked some of his friends to help him to buy reindeer from Northern Europe for breeding in Labrador. The money was obtained and help was given by the Canadian Government. Three hundred reindeer were bought in Lapland and large quantities of moss were collected for their food on the long voyage across the Atlantic. Once the voyage had begun, drinking water was a problem. Reindeer will not drink still water and it was necessary to build an imitation waterfall to make them feel at home. Their lovely antlers had to be cut off as they would have got in the way in the confined space on the ship's deck. It was a pity, because, without their beautiful horns, the deer did not look such fine animals, but it did not greatly matter as the horns would soon grow again.

When the steamer on which they travelled reached Newfoundland, it was winter time. The sea was frozen over and the reindeer had to be lowered on to the ice. Many of them fell through cracks into the sea, but they managed to reach the shore without a single one being lost.

Three families of Laplanders had travelled with the reindeer, to look after them on the journey, and to teach the Eskimos how to look after the herd. One of the Lapp women injured a leg on the voyage and had to go into the Mission hospital. When she reached the hospital it was seen that she had brought with her, her most precious possession—a frying pan!

For a time the herd did very well. In five years the 300 increased to 1,500. But then began a series of troubles. The Laplanders, unfortunately, did not settle happily in their new home. They complained that it was too cold and that they had to work too hard. They asked for more money than Doctor Grenfell felt the Mission could afford to pay. He, therefore, decided to let them go back to Lapland, although they warned him that without them he would not keep the deer. They were right. Within a few years only 230 deer were left.

The chief cause of losses was poaching. A poacher is a man who trespasses on someone else's property in search of game. Each season hundreds of fishermen came up the coast from the South of Newfoundland; they landed, saw reindeer, and shot them. It would have been possible to catch some of the poachers and punish them, but Doctor Grenfell, who was himself a magistrate, found that to do so aroused so much bad feeling that it was just not worth the trouble. The Government was not willing to help him; they could not afford to build the long fences necessary. In the end, the Doctor decided to move the reindeer which were left. They were rounded up with some difficulty and taken to an island called Anticosti Island where they were allowed to run wild. It is an island about the size of Wales, which stands in the mouth of the St. Lawrence River and is used as a place where animals are preserved.

XIII

ADRIFT

In the year 1908 Doctor Grenfell experienced one of the most remarkable of all his many adventures. It began on Easter Sunday, April 21st, at the time of the year when the ice begins to break up and float Southwards until it melts in the warmer waters. He went to the morning service in the little church and was on his way back to the hospital when he was met by a boy, who ran up with the news that a large team of dogs had arrived from a place about sixty miles away where the doctor was urgently needed. The patient was a young man on whom an operation had been performed a few days before. The wound had been allowed to close, while there was poison inside his body. His condition had become serious and Doctor Grenfell knew that it might be necessary to take off a leg in order to save his life. In any case there was no time to be lost.

He set off at once, with a team of fresh husky dogs. By nightfall he had covered twenty miles and had reached a small village where it was decided to spend the night. The weather was most unpleasant, both fog and rain adding to the difficulties of travelling over the soft snow. Forty miles had to be covered the next day, ten of them over a frozen arm of the sea. The ice was beginning to break up and here and there were large cracks, but the doctor was in a great hurry and he did not think twice about taking his sledge over the ice. Suddenly, when he was within a quarter of a mile of the shore to which he was going, the wind dropped. The wind had been blowing towards the shore holding the ice up against the land. Now he saw that all around him the ice was loosening, and that he could not retreat to safety or reach the shore ahead.

Remembering that only a few weeks earlier a man had been drowned because he had been pulled under the water by the reins of his dogs entangled round him, Doctor Grenfell pulled out his sheath-knife and cut the traces, just keeping a rein from the leading dog fastened to his wrist. This dog climbed out of the water on to a piece of frozen snow, and something like a huge, floating snowball. The Doctor hauled himself along

through the water and had nearly reached the raft
of snow when the dog slipped out of the harness.
The cold was making him feel faint, when he
managed to catch hold of the rein of another dog
which had climbed on to a piece of ice and he
hauled himself out of the water beside the dog. He
was, however, on a very small piece of ice and it
was clear that he would soon be drowned if he could
not make his way to a larger ice-pan. A few yards
away was a pan large enough to last for some
hours and so provide a greater chance for him
to be seen and rescued. His problem was to
persuade the dogs to go to that pan of ice, carrying
the line along which he could haul himself to safety.
When he threw the dogs into the water they just
scrambled back on to the smaller piece of ice,
which was after all the only ice they could see
once they were in the water.

Then the doctor had an idea. As well as the
big Labrador dogs, he had with him his small
black spaniel, which was light enough to get
across to the larger ice pan without falling in. He
showed the spaniel the direction by throwing a
piece of ice towards the refuge. You all know how
dogs love to chase after anything that you throw
for them. The little black dog dashed after the bit
of ice and reached the pan safely. The larger dogs
could see the spaniel and understood where their
master wanted them to go. Next time they went
in they struggled to the ice pan, carrying the line,
along which the Doctor intended to haul himself.
This time he had tied the harness in such a way

that the dogs could not slip out of it and after a long struggle in the water he was able to drag himself on to the ice pan.

His position was still very dangerous. The pan was really only made up of numerous small pieces of floating ice frozen together. It would soon break up as it floated out to sea. He had left his warm clothes and thermos flask on the smaller piece of ice, together with his matches and wood. No one in living memory had ever gone adrift in that bay. There was very little chance of anyone seeing him. He had to think about protecting himself from the cold. He took off his knee-length boots and cut them down to the feet. Then he opened them out and fitted them round his back as a kind of jacket to protect himself from the wind. But this was not enough. He would freeze to death if he could not find warm covering. The only thing to do was to kill some of the dogs and cover himself with their skins. It was no easy matter, but he killed three of them, feeling, as he did so, almost envious of the dogs for their quick end, while he was probably going to experience a slow and unpleasant death.

His clothes were soaking wet. He took his garments off, wrung them out and put them on in turn next to his skin in the hope that they would be dried by the heat from his body. He piled up the carcasses of the three dogs and sheltered behind them from the wind. He then pulled to pieces the ropes of the dogs' harness and used them as wrappings round his feet in an effort to warm them.

And then he went to sleep! In the bitter cold
he nestled up close to his largest dog and obtained
just enough warmth to sleep for a short time. He
woke up shivering with the cold, but was glad to
find that the wind had dropped and that the sea
was calm. He slept again for a time and on next
waking up realized that he ought to fly some kind
of flag. That meant that he needed a flag pole. He
made one out of the bones from the legs of
the dogs he had killed, tied together with bits of
old harness rope, a very crooked flagpole, but one
which rose several feet above his head. As soon as
day dawned he took off his shirt—it was an old
football shirt—and tied it to the flagpole.

You may be wondering how Doctor Grenfell
was feeling all this time. At first, he had been too
busy keeping himself warm to think about anything else. He tells us that he knew no feelings of
fear. He even laughed at himself at the sight he
made, waving his flag towards a barren and
deserted coast in the distance. He faced death,
but it held no terrors for him. He believed, with
St. Paul, that Christ had removed the sting from
death, so that for those who follow Him death
becomes the gateway to Life. To his mind came
the words of an old hymn he had often sung:

"My God, my Father, while I stray
Far from my home on life's rough way,
Oh, help me from my heart to say,
Thy will be done."

Was it to be God's will that his life of usefulness
to the people of Labrador was to end in these cold

and icy waters? At any rate, the Doctor was not giving up hope. He was determined to try every means possible to attract attention. He had a few matches with him and he laid these out in the sun. He even tried to use a piece of transparent ice as a burning glass in the hope of starting a fire or at least causing some smoke. Once he thought that he saw the glitter of an oar in the distance, but he knew that it was very unlikely because there was so much floating ice about that it would have been extremely difficult to force a boat through it. In any case the bright snow had caused what is known as snow-blindness, the same sort of thing that happens to your eyes in the very bright sunshine that makes you want to wear sunglasses.

Later on, he thought the glitter of an oar was more distinct, but still he did not trust his eyesight. Eventually, the oar came near enough for him to see that there really was a boat, and to know that if his ice held for another hour he would be rescued. At last, as the boat came nearer, he could see his rescuers waving wildly. They shouted to him to stay where he was and not to get excited. But, as a matter of fact, it was the rescuers who were most excited and the doctor certainly had no wish to plunge into the icy water again.

When the boat came up close to the ice-pan, one of the men jumped on to the ice and shook the Doctor's hand. Neither of them spoke a word. It was one of those occasions when no words would have conveyed the depth of joy which both must have felt. He handed the Doctor a flask of hot tea.

Soon Doctor and dogs were aboard the boat and it was pushing its way back through the floating ice.

It turned out that the previous evening four men had been cutting up seals when one of them thought he saw something alive on the ice. They hurried to their village and made straight for the house of the man who owned a small telescope. He left his supper and ran to the cliffs, from which through the darkening shadows he could just make out the form of a man drifting on a piece of ice. They guessed that the man was their beloved Doctor and as soon as daylight began to dawn the rescue expedition set out. It meant a dangerous trip through heavy breakers.

We can imagine the scene as the boat arrived back at the village. Every man, woman and child came down to the shore to shake the Doctor by the hand. It must have hurt his hands for they were badly frost-bitten. He was still wearing the blood-covered skins of the dogs and was tied around with rags, stuffed out with the shredded ropes.

After this adventure he had to spend a few days in bed, to recover from the effects of the bitter cold on his hands and feet. He did not forget the dogs and in the hallway of his home he had a bronze tablet put, with these words

To the Memory of Three Noble Dogs.

MOODY

WATCH

SPY

whose lives were given for mine on the ice

April 21st, 1908

The lad whose life Doctor Grenfell had been trying to save was brought to the hospital by boat and was soon on the way to recovery.

I should like to finish the story by quoting the Doctor's own words. "We all love life," he wrote, "and I was glad to have a new lease of it before me. As I went to sleep that night there still rang through my ears the same verse of the old hymn which had been my companion on the ice-pan:

" 'Oh, help me from my heart to say,
    Thy will be done.' "

XIV

TWICE ONE!

THE year after this adventure, Doctor Grenfell came to England. He travelled all over the country, telling people in crowded meetings of the work in Labrador. When the time came for him to return there once more, he suddenly decided to take his mother with him. She was seventy-eight at the time, but she fell in with his plans and in June they sailed together on a famous liner called the *Mauretania*. She was at the time the fastest ship that had ever been made and on one day of that very voyage she travelled further than any ship had ever done before in twenty-four hours.

The voyage was memorable however, in Doctor Grenfell's career, for quite a different reason. Until then he had been far too busy with his work to think about getting married. Now, on this voyage, he met the lady who was to become his wife. The ship was travelling at top speed. This meant that he had not much time to get to know her and ask the all-important question. At first he only knew her as "the lady in black" and when he asked her to marry him she reminded him that he did not even know her name! "The only thing that interests me," he answered, "is what it is going to be!"

She was an American girl by the name of Anne MacClanahan. Her ancestors had come from Scotland. She lived with her mother—her father had died—near to Lake Michigan, one of those great and beautiful lakes which you can find on your atlas between Canada and the United States. As soon as he could, Doctor Grenfell visited her at her home, met his future mother-in-law and took up horse-riding for the first time for many years. The wedding was arranged for November of the year 1909 and took place in Chicago. A few weeks later he took his bride to Labrador. Fortunately, she was a good sailor, for as they sailed up the coast they met a strong head wind and a snow blizzard which caused their boat to take nine days instead of four, while the snow covered the vessel until it looked like a floating Christmas cake.

You know in arithmetic that twice one equals two; but Doctor Grenfell said he had found that twice one made more than two. He meant that in partnership with his wife more had been done than two people could have done separately. God blessed their marriage with three children, two boys and a girl, the girl being the youngest of the three.

Mrs. Grenfell had once refused the chance to attend a lecture on Labrador by a medical missionary. Now that she was married to the missionary she spent herself gladly in the noble cause they both had at heart. Her home was an open house, where visitors were always welcome. Each year she acted as mother to groups of boys and girls, who were to receive further education in Canada and the United States.

Then she thought over a problem that was always cropping up—how to obtain all the money that was needed to keep the fine work going. Neither she nor her husband liked to be always begging for money. Why should they not earn the money they needed?

One day she had a splendid idea. Everybody uses calendars. They buy them each year to give to their friends at Christmas time. Why should they not produce a better calendar than anyone else and sell it on behalf of the work?

An original picture was painted for them by the artist who designed the King's Christmas card. A famous art publisher took the work in hand and 20,000 copies were printed. Not all were sold, but the 3,500 copies left over were framed and sold as souvenirs. Several thousand pounds were raised for the Mission.

Another of her ideas was the Dog-Team Tavern. This was a place on one of the busiest

American highways, where funds were raised by selling to tourists the things which the fishermen of Labrador were making during the months of the year when they could not go out fishing. Teas were served to the customers and all the necessary work was done by volunteers, that is, people who gave their time gladly without any payment or reward except to know that they were helping with a great piece of Christian work.

Much of Doctor Grenfell's time was spent in giving lectures on the work. In doing this he made long tours of Great Britain, Canada and the United States. He found such tours much more tiring than the actual work in Labrador, but they gave him some amusing experiences. Once he found himself standing between a lady and gentleman at a crowded gathering. He could not remember either of their names, but thought he ought to introduce them to each other. Turning to the gentleman he said, "Please let me present you to Mrs. M—m—m—" "Oh don't trouble," the gentleman replied, "We've been married for thirty years!"

Travelling by train, once the Doctor was asked how he had liked Toleda. He replied that he had never been there. "Strange," murmured his questioner, "because you spent two days in my house!"

He became so used to shaking hands with people that at a railway station he shook hands with the ticket collector instead of showing his ticket!

In the city of St. John's in Newfoundland there was no place to which fishermen could go when their vessels were in port. Doctor Grenfell was anxious that some building should be put up where seamen could meet their friends, play games and stay until they sailed again. A large building was needed and this meant that a large sum of money had to be found.

By 1911 most of the required sum had been raised and it was decided to start building. The King, George V, was deeply interested in the work—he had himself spent so much of his life at sea that he was known as the Sailor King—and he promised that if the Mission would arrange for a direct line from St. John's to Buckingham Palace, he would press a button which would set moving the machinery that would place the stone in position. Arrangements were made by the Telegraph Company and on the day of his Coronation, following the ceremony in Westminster Abbey, the King, from a distance of 3,000 miles, laid the foundation stone of the new Institute.

About this time Doctor Grenfell was given a fine three-masted schooner by an American gentleman, Mr. Cluett. It had been suggested that a suitable text for inscription on the vessel would be the verse from one of the Psalms which tells us, "The sea is His and He made it." When the ship arrived the doctor was rather surprised, however, to find that the bronze tablet read: "This vessel with full equipment was presented by George B. Cluett to Wilfred T. Grenfell. The sea is His and He made it." It is a good example of how careful you need to be when you use words like "He" and "His" to make sure that it is quite clear to whom they refer.

Just before the outbreak of the 1914-18 war, Doctor Grenfell and his wife, on a well-deserved holiday, visited a number of countries they had never been to before. In Greece they were deeply interested to find themselves among scenes familiar to the great pioneers of civilization of whom you hear in your history lessons. In Athens they stood on Mars Hill, where the Apostle Paul once proclaimed the Gospel of God's love for all His children; in another place well-known to St. Paul, Ephesus, Doctor Grenfell found that the once great city was a heap of ruins. The only inhabitant to be found there was a donkey.

At Pergamos he stayed with a Greek family who showed him a famous national dance in which those taking part disappear one by one. It is danced in memory of some brave Greek girls who danced to the edge of a precipice over which they threw themselves in turn rather than be captured by enemies and forced into slavery.

At the time of Doctor Grenfell's visit, Greece was an occupied country, under the rule of the Turks who had been there for about four hundred years. One result of the 1914-18 war was that Greece became free once more.

In Labrador that summer, the most memorable event was the visit of the Duke of Connaught Governor-General of Canada, and son of Queen Victoria. Before landing himself, he sent a band ashore, knowing that the people in Labrador had

never heard a band. Unfortunately they mistook
the leader of the band in his fine uniform for the
Duke and welcomed him far more warmly than the
gentleman in ordinary clothes who was the first
member of the Royal family to set foot there.
Doctor Grenfell thinks they may have felt something like the little boy who met him, a real
knight, but was disappointed because he had left
his armour at home!

During the early part of the war, the Doctor
spent a time in France, working on the
battlefields, until more doctors came forward for
this work and he felt that he was more needed in
Labrador.

XV

HELP FOR THE SEAFARER

WE are so used to the postman making his daily
call that we should certainly miss him if he
stayed away for months at a time. The people of
Labrador were at one time cut off from their
friends through the winter. They heard no news
of the outside world and received no letters. The
invention of radio changed all that, making it
possible for them to know the news as speedily as
anywhere else in the world.

Few men have ever dared to try to cross the
Straits of Belle Isle, separating Labrador from
Newfoundland, during the months when the
Straits are packed with huge masses of ice, driven

by fierce gales and heaving waters into what Doctor Grenfell described as "one of the wildest sights of Nature". One who risked his life to get across, however, was the postman. After several successful crossings, even he realized that it was foolish to make a regular habit of hazarding his life in that fearful place.

The number of shipwrecks each year was a cause of great anxiety to Doctor Grenfell. Very often it was possible to haul the wrecked ship off the rocks on which it had foundered, but not possible to sail it several hundred miles to a dry dock where it could be repaired. The loss of so many valuable vessels in turn meant the loss of food and great hardship and hunger. Just as he believed that Christ had sent him to preach the Gospel and to heal the sick, so he believed that he should do something to save the ships and thus prevent the hardship brought about by their loss. An appeal was made for funds and an anonymous donor (somebody who gives money, but does not allow anyone to find out who he is) paid for a dry dock, into which ships could be hauled and repaired. Each year it was the means of saving several vessels which otherwise would have been total losses.

Another task which Doctor Grenfell felt he should tackle was the preparation of accurate charts of the Labrador coast. He realized that Christians should be always ready to help the the widows and children of brave fishermen who lost their lives. But how much better if they could

prevent the loss of such lives by making good maps
on which dangerous rocks and sandbanks would
be clearly marked. All this was included in his
task of preaching the Gospel.

Before he could begin, however, money had to be
found to pay for the cost. Those who were raising
money for the Mission could not spare any for a
survey expedition. As the doctor thought about it
he remembered a limerick he had once heard,

> "There was a young lady said, 'Why
> Can't I see down my ear with my eye?
> If I put my mind to it,
> I surely can do it;
> You never can tell till you try.'"

It was only a nonsense rhyme, but it made him
realize that if he put his mind to it, he might find
a way to obtain the money.

A friend of his, an American doctor, owned a
small plane, which he was willing to lend. Other
help came from various quarters. One firm gave
10,000 gallons of petrol another 1,000 gallons of
oil. A shipping company provided free passages for
five workers from England, who were to help with
the survey. Preparation of the chart was under-
taken by the Geographical Society of New York.

From the plane many hundreds of photographs
were taken. By putting these together it was
possible to make an accurate chart of the country.
Then, on the water, soundings were carefully
made to discover the depth of the sea, so that all
shallow places could be clearly shown.

The whole experience encouraged Doctor

Grenfell in his belief that Labrador was not quite such a useless waste as the early discoverers had imagined. On the other hand, he believed that the land could be made to produce more food and that the region could attract holiday makers to see its beautiful fjords, waterfalls and icebergs, during the summer months when the sun shines at midnight.

Another way in which the people of Labrador are helped is through a fund which provides money to those who suffer sudden and unexpected loss such as the sinking of their fishing boats. The missionaries are responsible for giving money from this fund whenever they feel there is need for help.

The people of Labrador had to be taught that Nature's gifts must be used with great care. Like many other peoples in the world they were using up what they had without any thought of provision for the future. Only by hard work and much careful planning do men fill their larders. In Holland they build dykes to guard their fields from the invading sea. On the steep hillsides of Italy they carve out terraces on which they grow grapes, olives and other fruits. But in some lands trees are recklessly cut down to provide wood for fires, even though it means that desert sands advance where the trees have been and swallow up good food-producing soil.

Much of the poverty of Labrador was due to the ignorant using up of Nature's gifts without planning for the future. You know enough about

Doctor Grenfell by now to realize that he would regard it as more important to show people how to grow plenty of food than to go on year after year giving food to the hungry.

The trouble with Labrador was that the summer was too short for plants to grow to their best. The ground is frozen over until July. Seeds planted then will not grow into very large plants before the wintry weather sets in. "Very well, then," said the doctor, "we must give them longer." How? By growing the seeds under glass, so that in July it is possible to plant out three-month old plants. So successful was the first effort at growing green vegetables that cabbages weighing up to eighteen pounds were produced. When the people saw these huge cabbages they were delighted, and, in the following year, bought 15,000 plants grown in the greenhouse to plant out in their own gardens.

Unfortunately, there were pests and diseases in Labrador just as in other parts of the world. Help was given by an American professor who went there at his own expense to study their problems and advise them how to destroy the pests which would otherwise ruin their crops.

The value of all the efforts made was proved one year when the fishing proved so bad that the people would have starved to death or had to live on gifts of food sent to them had it not been for the produce of their gardens.

I have already referred to the usefulness of trees and of the foolishness of those who cut them down without planting more to replace them. It was a great temptation to the people of Labrador to cut down their few trees for firewood and logs. Even the passing of laws and the sending to prison of those who cut down trees did not stop them.

Doctor Grenfell saw that some other kind of fuel must be found and tried hard to persuade the people to burn peat. Peat is decayed vegetable matter which is dried and used for fuel in some countries, particularly in Ireland. It was a long time, however, before the people could be persuaded that peat was as good as wood for keeping their homes warm.

Many of the people were so poor that the Mission had to lend them money to buy the tools and seed they needed, as well as to obtain sea-boots, fishing tackle and paint for their boats. The fishermen were not often able to repay the money, but discharged their debts by working in the gardens of the nearest nursing station.

The keeping of farm animals in Labrador was difficult because of the wildness of the dogs. The only solution seemed to be to keep the dogs shut up. A law was passed under which dogs were to be destroyed if found loose during the summer months. It was hard on the dogs and the Mission again stepped in to help the poor people to buy the wire and nails they needed to make proper enclosures, the dogs being much too large to be kept in kennels.

A friend of the work paid for the building of

kennels at one of the Mission stations, where the dogs could be boarded out. They were built close to the sea, where the tide would come into the runways and give the dogs a chance to keep themselves clean.

Attempts at cross-breeding with dogs of milder temper, such as sheepdogs and wolf-hounds, have been made, but without success. Nor did the dogs used to Greenland prove suitable when introduced to Labrador. They became victims of a disease which made it unsafe to keep them.

With the dogs shut up it was found possible to keep cows, sheep and pigs successfully. Scottish sheep with black faces were introduced because they were a breed of sheep which could be fattened on heather. They adapted themselves to Labrador by eating nearly all the wild plants found there.

Another experiment made was the introduction of bees, which the local people had never seen before. At first they were worried about who would have to take the food to the bees each day! They did well for a time and stored up a good deal of honey. Unfortunately no one knew much about bees and it was not realized until too late that the bees were using up their winter store of honey much too quickly.

Yet another experiment tried was the preservation of food. We are all used to the idea of obtaining some of our meals from tins or bottles. An expert in the art of canning visited two of the Mission stations one summer to hold classes for the fishermen's wives, at which they taught the whole process of canning fish and local berries. At first they were a bit suspicious but they soon found that it was a cheap way of storing up food for the winter. One result of this was that one of the Labrador girls went to an American college, specially to learn the art of preserving food.

A girl in the American city of Chicago who was interested in helping Doctor Grenfell's work hit upon the idea of sending goats to Labrador to provide fresh milk for the babies and young children who needed it. She asked people to help her to provide goats in every Labrador village. Eight goats were given and the doctor was told that they were being sent to him by rail and ship. Now they were very valuable goats, worth more than £100 each and he was afraid they might come to harm on the way. He appealed, therefore, for volunteers to bring the goats and ensure that they received the best care and attention. The result was that eight girls came forward to travel by steamer with the goats.

The animals settled down well and provided the required milk. They also enjoyed themselves in the local gardens, which lacked fences strong enough to keep the goats out. Because of this damage to the gardens, the people were not too keen on the goats and they were replaced as soon as possible by cows.

Several kinds of berries are grown in Labrador. Blueberries, which grow to the size of small grapes, are sweet and are easily picked. They are plentiful enough for some to be exported to the United States. They are not spoiled by the cold. In fact they thrive on it; the soil of Newfoundland is particularly suitable for them. Other fruits grown there are cranberries, red apples and yellow apples, suitable for baking. In some parts of Newfoundland raspberries grow wild.

XVI

HEAL THE SICK

FROM its earliest days, the Christian Church has realized that healing and care of the sick is one of its most important tasks. When Jesus sent his disciples out into the villages of Palestine, He told them to "heal the sick" wherever they went. Of our Lord Himself we are told that "He healed them that had need of healing." His followers all down through the ages have taken a leading part in the building of hospitals and the study of medicine.

Only sixty years ago there was no hospital in Labrador. Nor was there a doctor nor nurses. It was this sorry state of affairs that Doctor Grenfell set out to change. He lived to see the establishment of four hospitals and five nursing stations along the coast. The hospitals are widely separated; some patients would have no hope of reaching them in time to receive the attention they need if it were not for the nursing stations. If you try to imagine hospitals as far apart as London, Sheffield, Glasgow and Aberdeen, you may be able to realize what a problem it was deciding exactly where the hospitals were most needed and could be most useful.

Before the nursing station was established at Flowers Cove, the Doctor was passing through here when a young man was brought in with a bad leg injury, caused by his gun going off in his boat. Caught without his medical instruments, the Doctor used an ordinary thread to control the bleeding, then cut off the lad's leg with his pocket knife. The patient was taken to a nursing station at Forteau where he was carefully nursed until he had made a full recovery. Today there is a nursing station at Flowers Cove. The nurses there often have to walk ten to twenty miles a day to visit their patients.

Other examples of cases brought in to the station at Forteau were a man who had shot off his arm and a six-year-old boy who had mistakenly swallowed boiling water. Between the Mission hospital at Harrington and the nursing station at Forteau was an area across which it was impossible to travel during the winter. It was therefore decided to establish a nursing station in this area at a place called Mutton Bay. Poor though the fishing folk were, they promised to provide a home and food for the nurse, and also make it possible for her to get about to visit her patients.

Sometimes during the winter months, when you are enjoying yourselves in the snow or grousing about the cold, spare a thought for those brave nurses who have chosen to spend their lives in such lonely, bleak outposts; and pray that God will help them and watch over them in all they do for the people of Labrador.

So deeply moved was Doctor Grenfell by the self-sacrifice of these fine Christian women that he used to say he wished he could write great poetry like Tennyson so that he could describe their wonderful work in the way that the poet pays tribute to Grenville of the *Revenge* (an ancestor of Grenfell's).

Further south in Newfoundland was another needy area. At a place called Twillingate in Notre Dame Bay lives were being lost because of the great distances to a hospital. Naturally the people were eager to have a hospital in their midst, but the Government of Newfoundland was slow to offer help.

One day the mail steamer brought to the Mission hospital at St. Anthony an elderly, white-haired seaman, with a fine, noble face, but obviously in great pain. He had come from Notre Dame Bay, where he had waited for months for the first steamer of the season to take him to the hospital for treatment. The vessel had been delayed on its voyage by the large amounts of ice still blocking the channel and there was no one on board to care properly for the patient. When Doctor Grenfell saw the man's condition he left him to be carried to the hospital on a stretcher, while he hurried ahead to make sure there would not be a moment's delay in attending to him. But the journey had proved too much for the old chap and he was beyond the help of the Doctor when the stretcher reached the door of the hospital. From that moment Doctor Grenfell determined that, whether the Government helped or not, there should be a hospital at Notre Dame Bay.

Shortly after this incident a gift of several thousand pounds was sent to the mission. The Doctor decided at once to use it for the establishment of the hospital at Twillingate. An American doctor took over the responsibility and local girls were trained as nurses. When the Government at last saw how greatly the hospital was needed they offered a yearly grant to keep it going.

Sometimes a doctor finds a case which is too difficult for him to deal with. Then he calls in another doctor who has made a special study of particular diseases or of illnesses which affect particular parts of the body. These men are known as specialists and there are many kinds of them—eye specialists, lung specialists, nose and throat specialists and so on. In a country like Britain there are specialists in every large town and it does not take long to get one if you are unfortunate enough to need him.

Most of them have to work very hard. Because their work is so valuable, it is possible for them to earn large fees, but when Doctor Grenfell asked some of them to visit Labrador, they not only went, but paid their own expenses. These men knew of the sacrifices made by the doctors and nurses working in Labrador and were glad to give whatever help they could. The example of those who show love for their neighbours (according to Jesus, your neighbour is anyone who needs your help) inspires others to deeds of love and kindness.

No character in the world's history has so inspired deeds of love and self-sacrifice as the Good Samaritan who went to the help of the man who had been robbed. Commenting on this story, Doctor Grenfell wrote: "A doctor of medicine expresses his love for his neighbour by crossing the road to attend to his physical wounds, rather than by hurrying to Jerusalem to say prayers for his benefit."

Many generous friends of the work have sent the Doctor their gifts, without which its continuation would not be possible. He once stayed with a gentleman who, as a young man, had visited the Labrador coast and had nearly been left behind there. When his ship sailed away the local people had showed him great kindness, giving him oilskin clothing which in those days was very costly in that part of the world. He made his way along the coast and was able to rejoin his ship, but he never forgot the kindness he had been shown. More than forty years he waited for a chance to repay it. Then he gave Doctor Grenfell enough money to build a house for a nurse at Forteau. This nursing station is about halfway between two of the hospitals, Battle and Harrington, and has been of untold blessing to people in the locality.

Many of the diseases common in Labrador were caused by lack of proper food and clothing. To buy the food and clothes needed to improve their health, the people had to have money. Especially they needed interesting work, which could bring them in a steady income during the months of the year when they could not be fishing or trapping. The lives of the women were particularly dull. Most of their time was spent indoors, providing for the needs of their large families.

This need for interesting and profitable work led Doctor Grenfell to teach the people new trades and handicrafts. Rug-making was an ideal industry with which to begin, for it was a craft which ancestors from the fishing folk of Scotland, Devon and Cornwall had known and had passed on to their children. Worn-out clothes were turned into floor coverings for their cottages. If rugs were to be made for sale elsewhere, new materials had to be obtained for the people to use. The Mission arranged for these materials and were rewarded by seeing some beautiful rugs made.

Other crafts which were encouraged and developed included pottery, basket weaving and bead work. Expenses have been kept down by using all kinds of things for materials. Old silk stockings, for example, can be turned into attractive mats. This gave rise to the slogan, "When your stocking begins to run, let them run to Labrador!" Many stockings which would normally have been thrown into the rag bag have found their way across the ocean to begin a new life of usefulness underfoot instead of around peoples' feet!

When folk are ill and have to spend a long time

in hospital, they recover more quickly if they have something interesting to do. Thus arose the need to find suitable occupation for the patients, crafts which could be carried out by those in bed.

Toy making was one thing they could do. Patients would carve wooden animals or dog teams pulling sledges which were exact models of the real thing. The toy sledges were made in the same ways as the long komatiks, the pieces being lashed together, not nailed.

Whaling companies, knowing how useful the Mission would find ivory, gave them quantities of whales' teeth. These together with the ivory tusks of walruses and narwhals are carved into attractive sets of chessmen or figures of Eskimos, seals, bears, dogs, and igloos, all of which can be sold easily, especially when people realize that they have actually been made in Eskimo land.

The jacket which is most commonly worn in the winter is made of a special cloth which is both light and warm, as well as being proof against rain, wind and snow. It is known as Grenfell cloth, the name given to it by the firm which developed its manufacture after the Doctor had requested that they should experiment to find a material which had those qualities. Using this cloth, the people make the jackets—dickeys they call them—trim them with fur and embroider them in bright colours. They find a ready sale in winter sports centres in America.

For men, women and children recovering from illness, such work is better than medicine.

It helps them to keep their minds off their troubles and enables them to feel less helpless and dependent on others for everything.

Sometimes the cost of materials may be more than the finished work will sell for. Some people will say that it is not worth doing. But to the staff of the Mission it is as worth while as saving some-one's life when it might cost less to let them die and have only the funeral expenses to pay.

The money which comes through the sale of mats enables the people to buy clothes they need for the bitter winter. It would not now be possible for anyone to be so poorly clad as one little girl who in the early days of the work walked barefooted to the Mission simply because she had no shoes or stockings. Moreover she wore only a cotton frock, for she had no warm coat, although the temperature was twenty degrees below freezing point.

At the Wembley Exhibition in 1924 the Grenfell Association had a stall at which the work produced in Labrador and Newfoundland was sold. Queen Mary was one of the customers who purchased items to add to her wonderful collec-tion of curios from all parts of the world.

When the old original orphanage building had been so battered by the winter storms that it became unfit for children to live in, it was turned into an Industrial Building, where the various crafts I have told you about could be carried on. It was not an ideal building for the purpose, as snow drifted in at almost every window and the roof leaked badly;

but so many wanted to work there that there was just not room for all of them.

These industries are still flourishing and there is a ready sale for the goods among men stationed at the air bases which have been established out there in recent years.

XVII

EASTERN INTERLUDE

IN 1924 the Doctor and his wife set off on a tour round the world. After more than thirty years in the sub-Arctic climate of Labrador, a visit to warmer lands was a pleasant change. Crossing Europe to Trieste, they sailed from there to Alexandria and then southwards to see the wonderful Pyramids, built by men when first they learned to use stone for building, and remaining through 5,000 years the most massive buildings ever put up. They were old when Moses was hidden among the bulrushes. Beside them is the famous Sphinx, gazing silently towards the vast desert of the Sudan. Wherever the Doctor went, crowds of men and boys were yelling for money, "a plague of Egypt," he said, not mentioned in the "book of Exodus". They reminded him as they scrambled for coins of the Eskimo dogs fighting one another for bones.

From Egypt they went to Palestine, where they visited many of the places we read of in our Bibles. He travelled on the road from Jerusalem to Jericho, where our Lord must have often been and where the Good Samaritan performed the act which has made him so famous. Doctor Grenfell bathed in the Dead Sea, so salty and buoyant that he was able to lie on his back in the water while he ate an apple and read a book.

Next he travelled on eastwards across the desert to the ruins of Babylon, a city built with walls so wide that two four-horsed chariots could pass abreast at full speed. He found that what had once been a great centre of civilisation was in the twentieth century a filthy and evil-smelling place, where the germs of disease lurked in every corner.

Ur of the Chaldees, where Abraham once lived, he found to be just a heap of sand in the centre of nowhere.

To Doctor Grenfell the once great land of Iraq seemed like a vast ocean of flat dried-up mud. It was with feelings of relief that he left it behind and sailed from Basra, for India. Here he felt more at home. It was the land in which his mother had been born and in which many of his relatives had served. He could not help contrasting India with Labrador. In India he could swim in the warm waters; there was no need for warm clothes or fires; nearly every useful kind of wood in the world could be grown there; it seemed that there was hardly a vegetable or fruit which could not be produced if wanted. In Delhi, he met Mr. Gandhi, one of the greatest men India, or indeed, the world has known.

It was with genuine regret that he left India.

The few weeks spent there were among the happiest of his life. He described the people as "capable, lovable and honest." He believed that they could have had far greater influence in the world were it not for the superstitions connected with the ancient religions of their land.

The next country he visited was China, where he sailed 800 miles up the Yangtze-Kiang river, fourth largest river in the world. He was over-joyed to find that wherever he went in that vast land he found a Mission hospital or school making known the Christian way of life. Many of these were in the hands of well-educated and capable Chinese Christian leaders.

He found the climate of Korea pleasant and the people polite and gentle. Dominated then by Japan, Doctor Grenfell expressed the hope that its future would be happy. He would have been sad to know of the terrible war which has ravaged the country in the last few years.

After the filth and evil smells of most eastern lands, it was an agreeable change to find in Japan that almost everybody, even the poorest, appeared to have a daily hot bath. While visiting the shrine of the Buddha, more than 1,000 years old, Doctor Grenfell caught sight of a rare type of butterfly. He had a butterfly net with him and at once gave chase. The crowd of Buddhist pilgrims were suddenly treated to the unusual sight of an English traveller, nearly sixty years of age, chasing a butterfly with the enthusiasm of a schoolboy. They were too polite, however, to show any amusement, even when the chase ended in the Doctor landing on all fours in a very muddy pond!

He was deeply impressed by the hard work of the Japanese and the way in which they were ready to engage in new kinds of work. He recorded that they were growing more food per acre than any other country in the world and expressed the wish that the people of Newfoundland would follow their example.

XVIII

THE KING REMEMBERS LABRADOR

MANY of the great men you read about in your history books and hear about at school lived their lives unhonoured and unrewarded for the benefits they gave to their fellow men. Not a few of them died in poverty and were buried in such obscurity that even their last resting place is not known. It is good to know that in modern times we have been quicker to recognize true greatness and to honour those who have spent their lives in the service of others.

To Doctor Grenfell came many great honours. None did he value more highly than the award of the Livingstone Gold Medal by the Royal Scottish Geographical Society. David Livingstone had been his lifelong hero and he was thrilled to have this link with one who like him was a doctor, explorer and Christian missionary.

One memorable day in the Doctor's career was

July 25th, 1927. On that day, in the most
Northerly corner of Newfoundland, a fine new
hospital was opened. The Governor General of
Newfoundland performed the opening ceremony
and several distinguished persons were present
for the occasion, but Doctor Grenfell himself
nearly missed it.

He was sailing Southwards in the hospital ship
Strathcona II after the first trip of the season along
the Labrador coast. On board were a number of
patients, including an aged blind fisherman. The
vessel was making headway in a dense fog when
it suddenly heeled over so sharply that Doctor
Grenfell and his crew were nearly thrown into
the sea. Water came pouring in, so that they
thought there must be a large hole in the side.
Fortunately they were able to launch the two
lifeboats and everyone managed to scramble into
them. Because of the thick fog the two boats soon
lost sight of each other.

After some hours Doctor Grenfell and his
companions were amazed to hear a bell ringing,
which they recognized as the bell of the *Strathcona*.
Making their way through the fog towards the
sound of the bell they were still more amazed to
see their little ship afloat, though very low in the
water because, of course, there was a great deal of
water in it. Alongside it was the other lifeboat.

Soon they had climbed on board and were
listening to the experiences of their friends. They,
too, had heard the ringing of the bell. Heading in
the direction from which the sound came they had

rowed within sight of the *Strathcona* when they saw a huge wave lift her off the rock and set her floating in deeper water. As soon as they had climbed on to the decks one of their number started ringing the bell to attract Doctor Grenfell's attention, while the others made themselves busy with buckets, baling out the water. Even the blind fisherman did his share.

So much water had been shipped that it was a long time before they could see any result from their effort. But, after much hard toil, the level of the water went down enough for them to light the fires again and raise steam to work the pump. To their great joy they found that the vessel was leaking very little. Most of the water had come in over the side when it had so suddenly heeled over.

It was still foggy, so that it seemed unlikely that they would reach St. Anthony in time to be present at the opening of the hospital. It was decided, however, to take the risk and in the end the *Strathcona* limped into the harbour at St. Anthony just before the Governor arrived to open the hospital.

There was great excitement in the village as it prepared to welcome its important visitors. The local Girl Guides, the most Northerly company in the world, lined the wharf. One of the visitors was an admiral who had distinguished himself during the war by sinking a German submarine with a small gun.

It was at the opening ceremony that the Governor made known that he had received a

cable from King George V, creating Doctor
Grenfell a Knight Commander of the Order of
Saint Michael and Saint George. From then
onwards he was *Sir* Wilfred Grenfell, and his
friends were proud and glad that the King had
thus shown his interest in, and appreciation of,
the great work that had been done.

A number of universities on both sides of the
Atlantic honoured him in various ways. The
University of St. Andrews in Scotland chose him
as its Rector. It was an appropriate choice, for St.
Andrew was a fisherman himself and is looked
upon as the fishermen's Saint. He was also a soul-
winner, for he found his own brother, Peter, and
brought him to Jesus. Doctor Grenfell had
devoted his life to the finding of fishermen and
bringing them to Jesus.

XIX

SERVING OTHERS

MANY of those who have helped Doctor Grenfell
in Labrador have been voluntary helpers. That
means they were not paid a salary for their
services, but went there to give in the spirit of
their Master who taught that "it is more blessed
to give than to receive." They had given themselves the name of "wops." In the course of the
years many hundreds of these wops have gone
from Britain, America and other lands to help
their neighbours in the far North.

Some have made great sacrifices to get out there, paying all their own expenses, or working their passage, which means working on a ship as one of the crew in exchange for a free voyage. One of the first wops risked his life, diving into an icy sea to rescue two people who were drowning.

Another who went out there had fallen into the habit of drinking heavily so that he was ruining his health. His brother, a famous surgeon, arranged for him to go to Labrador, where the temptation to drink would be removed, as no alcoholic drinks were allowed at any of the stations. He stayed for three years and when he went back to his business again he was in perfect health and cured of the habit which had been undermining it. There were others who went to recover from illness; we have already seen that a happily occupied person gets better more quickly than someone who had nothing to do.

The wops came from all kinds of homes. Some were the sons and daughters of millionaires, others from much poorer homes, and most from in between the two extremes. All were inspired by the chance to serve and help others.

A nurse who went out there only left them in order to go home and earn more money to get to Labrador again. A teacher sold doughnuts in a tea shop and made enough money at it to stay out there for eight years. A young lady painted pictures and then sold them to raise the funds to get out there. A medical student bred spaniels and sold them to pay his expenses.

At a large hospital in America half the nurses wanted to go to Labrador after Doctor Grenfell had visited their hospital. He had told them a remarkable story of a nurse who had gone to a lonely hamlet where there had been a serious outbreak of influenza. About a fortnight later she sent an urgent telegram to ask for help. A fisherman had become so ill with fever that he had not known what he was doing and had cut himself open with a sharp knife such as he used for cutting fish. The injury he had caused calmed his fever and he had gone straight to the nurse. In response to her call for help, the Doctor wired instructions and urged her to manage as best she could, for travel was impossible at the time. She called in the local priest who helped her to operate on the unfortunate patient. It was a task which normally would be done by an experienced surgeon. The operation was successful and the patient recovered. A few weeks later she brought him by boat over sixty miles to the hospital and he was back at work the following season.

A university undergraduate went to Labrador to help in the building of a house for needy children, paying for all the expense of the building. A carpenter from Kentucky went there at his own expense to teach the people how to make looms and wooden weaving apparatus. A lad lost a job which was offered to him because he stayed on in Labrador to finish some building work he had begun.

The wide variety of folk who helped Doctor

Grenfell made up what seemed to him like a modern band of Canterbury pilgrims. Their object was more useful to others than that of the old-time pilgrims. He said it would be easier to list the types which did *not* go than those which did. They had no gangsters or criminals offering to help; but doctors, scientists, lawyers, engineers, teachers, nurses, tradesmen of all kinds and girls from wealthy homes who had never needed to earn their living, all these were to be found among those who went on pilgrimage to Labrador. None of them asked for, nor expected, any reward other than the pleasure which comes from giving, whether the gift is in money or service.

Sometimes it has been possible for an aeroplane to prove its usefulness. At one lonely outpost on the Newfoundland coast, a place called Conche, the nurse had a patient in need of an urgent operation, which meant a journey to a Mission hospital forty miles away. Winter had set in and it was too late to make the journey by sea. Volunteers came forward, however, who offered to pull the patient to hospital by sledge, the journey over the hills being too difficult for dogs. It took them five-and-a-half days. That fact makes us realize how hard it must have been. Each time they stopped for a rest the nurse tended the sick man. At last he was brought safely to the hospital and a successful operation was performed.

The nurse's worries were not over, however. She had to get back to her post, where she might be needed by others. The owner of an aeroplane who was in town that day heard about her and offered to take her back in his plane. The return journey was done in twenty minutes. The nurse stepped out of the plane to find all the inhabitants of the village gathered in the open praying for her safe return.

The work which the wops have done is as varied as those who have done it. A university student drove Doctor Grenfell all over England on one of his lecture tours, thus saving him the expense of having a chauffeur. Perhaps the hardest work of all was done by those who went to Labrador to help with the making of roads, building bridges and wharves, and laying pipes which carry water to remote places. Among those who shared in these achievements were business men and university professors, men who were quite unused to such work, but who enjoyed the opportunity to serve their fellows.

xx

THE ADVENTURE GOES ON

LIFE in the open air is the finest medicine there is. Hard work is another, especially if that work is in the service of mankind. Sir Wilfred Grenfell continued his splendid work until 1935. He was then seventy, and the good health which he had enjoyed for so long began to fail at last. He had to retire. Even so he found the strength to visit

Labrador from time to time, the last occasion being in 1939, shortly before the outbreak of war. When he died in the following year, his tired body was laid to rest among the people to whom he had devoted more than forty years of his life. His grave on a hillside, overlooking St. Anthony, simply records his name and the dates of his birth and death. In Labrador and Newfoundland he will never be forgotten. He is still lovingly remembered by thousands whom he helped and healed.

Some of you will have read Tennyson's poem, "*The Revenge*", which is about Sir Wilfred's ancestor, Sir Richard Grenville. Some of the things which Tennyson wrote about the brave sailor who in the days of the first Queen Elizabeth defied fifty-three Spanish warships in his little vessel, *Revenge*, might very well apply to his equally brave descendant.

> "Sir Richard bore in hand all his sick
> men from the land . . .
> For we brought them all aboard,
> And they blest him in their pain."

There were those who laughed at Sir Wilfred and his "mad little craft" as the Spanish sailors had laughed long before at Sir Richard. But in both cases the laughter changed to admiration at the great courage which kept on fighting in the face of overwhelming odds.

The fight for better conditions in Labrador had needed a man with great courage and perseverance to lead it. When Sir Wilfred retired, enough had been done to make sure that the work would carry on. To-day, more than sixty years after he first sailed up the coast, the work goes on in four hospitals, five nursing stations and three boarding schools.

The people of Labrador are needing help to-day as much as ever. The last few years have seen the increase of a very serious disease called tuberculosis. Often people get this disease without knowing it. Maybe, when they find out, it is too late to cure them. For that reason it is necessary to take X-ray photographs of people who appear to be quite healthy to make sure that the disease is not beginning in them. The hospital ship has been equipped with X-ray apparatus for this purpose and the information which the doctors get from the photographs is enabling them to save many lives.

At St. Anthony a building for fifty beds has been added to the hospital, specially for people suffering from this disease. Another hospital and two new nursing stations have been built recently to take the place of buildings which were tumbling down. Even while this book is being written a new hospital is being built at North-West-River far in the North in the land of the Eskimos.

The schools run by the Mission are full. They are preparing for life, boys and girls who otherwise would grow up in almost complete ignorance, unable to read or write.

The industrial work is going on well. Each year more and more goods made in Labrador and

Newfoundland are finding their way to other parts of the world. The sale of beautifully made baskets is enabling the Labrador women to buy proper clothes for their families.

The Grenfell Association was the first organisation to teach other crafts to the fishing folk. Now they rejoice to see a measure of prosperity coming to these people. In the summer of 1954 a railway line 360 miles long was completed. This line links a remote inland district with the coast. On it will travel loads of iron ore from the last known reserve of this mineral in the whole North American continent. The deposit was discovered in an area inhabited only by the black bears. For several years it had been suspected that there might be enough iron ore in the frozen North to make the mining of it worthwhile. The building of the railway has taken several years.

Everything that was needed by the men on it had to be brought into the country, except water. Much came in by air. The work was made more difficult by extremely heavy rain.

In a year or two's time it is expected that 10,000,000 tons of iron ore will be carried yearly from the remote interior of Labrador to the great steel factories of the United States. It will mean that the people of Labrador, who have known poverty for so long, will have a greater share of the good things which make life pleasanter and happier.

Meanwhile the Mission is continuing the efforts begun by Doctor Grenfell to produce more food

locally. At North-West-River, carrots, cabbages
and potatoes are being grown in abundance.
Many of the Eskimos there have their own
gardens and grow most of what they need in them.
At St. Anthony in Northernmost Newfoundland,
the Mission's greenhouses are producing thousands of cabbage plants which they sell to the
local people at extremely low prices.

Plenty of milk is now available for the children
in the orphanage, for the Mission has a fine herd of
cows.   Calves and pigs are bred and sold to the
people to encourage their farming efforts.

The war years in Labrador were difficult. It
was almost impossible for volunteers to go out
there to help, but from 1946 onwards the flow of
these willing helpers began again. From both
sides of the Atlantic young people, looking for
adventure and a worthwhile piece of service,
made their way there, paying their own expenses.
The work they have done encourages those who
are spending their lives there. They are able to do
many things which the nurses and other workers
could never find time for, from the sawing up of
logs for winter fuel to the cutting of hay for the
cattle.

We are nearing the end of our story, a story of
one man's wonderful faith in God and his firm
belief that God wanted him to go to the help of
a people who were in the same position as the man
who was attacked by the thieves on the road from
Jerusalem to Jericho. Like him they needed
medical help; like him they needed a friend who

would care for them and give them a new start in life.

Sir Wilfred Grenfell was just the man for such an undertaking. The love for adventure was in his blood. As the Good Samaritan hastened to the side of the dying man, attended to his injuries and took care of him until he was on the road to recovery, so did Sir Wilfred hasten to the people of Labrador, to minister to their needs and to make provision for them to lead happier and easier lives. He would not like us to think too highly of him for what he did. He saw the task as his duty and he delighted in doing that duty. In the lips of his famous ancestor, Sir Richard Grenville, Tennyson has put the words:

> "I have fought for Queen and Faith like
>   a valiant man and true;
> I have only done my duty as a man is
>   bound to do;
> With a joyful spirit I, Sir Richard
>   Grenville, die!"

Sir Wilfred was a worthy son of the great Elizabethan sailor. Right valiantly he fought the good fight of faith for his Master and the people of Labrador and Northern Newfoundland. In that duty he found endless delight and adventure. In 1940 he embarked on the greatest adventure of all, but the work he began still flourishes. His spirit still inspires the workers in those bleak and lonely places. Whatever the future has in store for those peoples they will never forget the man who went among them as their first Doctor, gave them their first schools, cared for their orphans, encouraged the development of agriculture and handicraft, and preached to them "the old, old story of Jesus and His love."

POSTCRIPT

If any of you would like to hear more about the Grenfell Association and the latest news of the work in Labrador and Newfoundland, you should write to the Secretary, Grenfell Association of Great Britain & Ireland, 66 Victoria Street, Westminster, S.W.1.

Those of you who collect stamps might like to get some approvals from the Grenfell Stamp Bureau. The address is 88, Exeter House, Putney Heath, London S.W.15.